Jesus and Women

M. Adolorata Watson, OSM

One Liguori Drive
Liguori, Missouri 63057
(314) 464-2500

Imprimi Potest:
Stephen T. Palmer, C.SS.R.
Provincial, St. Louis Province
Redemptorist Fathers

Imprimatur:
+ Edward J. O'Donnell
Vicar General, Archdiocese of St. Louis

ISBN 0-89243-282-9
Library of Congress Catalog Card Number: 87-82947

Copyright © 1988, Liguori Publications
Printed in U.S.A.

All rights reserved. No part of this book may be reproduced, stored in a retrieval system, or transmitted without the written permission of Liguori Publications.

Scripture texts used in this work are taken from the NEW AMERICAN BIBLE copyright © 1970, with the REVISED NEW TESTAMENT copyright © 1986, by the Confraternity of Christian Doctrine, Washington, D.C., and are used by permission of copyright owner. All rights reserved.

Table of Contents

Introduction 5

1. Should She Work or Listen? 7
   Martha and Mary

2. Entering the House 11
   Peter's Mother-in-Law

3. Is She Dead or Alive? 15
   Jairus' Daughter

4. The Foolish and the Wise 21
   The Parable of the Ten Bridesmaids

5. "Who Touched Me?" 25
   A Woman With a Hemorrhage

6. Power of a Mother's Prayer 30
   The Possessed Girl

7. The Least is the Most 34
   The Poor Widow

8. The Search 37
   The Parable of the Woman and the Lost Coin

9. Women Are Disciples, Too 40
   Mary Magdalene, Joanna, Susanna

10. Compassionate Love 43
    A Widow and Her Dead Son

11. Winning the Case 47
    The Parable of the Widow and the Judge

12. "Who Let Her In?" 50
    A Sinful Woman

13. Present to the Beloved 55
    The Women at the Foot of the Cross

14. After the Resurrection 59
    Women Are the First to See the Risen Christ

Introduction

As we read the Good News of Jesus, we really listen to him speaking to us in the words of the Evangelists. The more we listen to Jesus, the more we realize that he tells us something above and beyond what the words themselves say. So it was for me as I pondered on the scenes in the Synoptic Gospels of Matthew, Mark, and Luke, especially those scenes and parables where women are the main characters.

The longer and the more deeply I reflected on these scenes and parables, the better I understood that Jesus was speaking to both men *and* women about the qualities of discipleship. As I listened to him in these parables and scenes, I heard him communicating with those of us who are his twentieth-century disciples. He was telling us that we should strive to live his message.

For that reason I want to share with others what it seems to me Jesus was saying to all his followers, then and now, through his meetings with women. Most of the accounts are brief, yet the message is clear. To be his followers we must show the same care and concern that he did in his ministry to others in need.

1
Should She Work or Listen?
Martha and Mary

In the movie *Yentl,* Barbra Streisand plays a young Jewish woman eager to learn the Torah (the Jewish Scriptures and tradition). To do so she must impersonate a man because women in that time and culture were not permitted to study such things. In Jesus' time, too, it was common thinking among Jewish men that women could not learn the Torah. The following scene is found only in Luke's Gospel where we are shown that Jesus did not follow the thinking of his time regarding women's ability to learn.

> As they continued their journey he entered a village where a woman whose name was Martha welcomed him. She had a sister named Mary [who] sat beside the Lord at his feet listening to him speak. Martha, burdened with much serving, came to him and said, ''Lord, do you not care that my sister has left me by myself to do the serving? Tell her to help me.'' The Lord said to her in reply, ''Martha, Martha, you are anxious and worried about many things. There is need of only one thing. Mary has chosen the better part and it will not be taken from her'' (Luke 10:38-42).

From what Luke writes, it seems that Jesus was accustomed to visiting the home of Martha and Mary, these sister-disciples of his. Perhaps their home was a center of teaching that Jesus had chosen. At that time, only men studied the Torah. The men would sit around a rabbi and discuss the meaning of the text. Women had no share in these mind-expanding and soul-transforming experiences. They were to learn from their husbands, if at all.

Surely Martha's request seems reasonable. Mary was enjoying relaxation while Martha busied herself with housework — probably the preparation of a meal. Of course, for one who enjoys cooking, the meal preparation might not seem like drudgery, but obviously Martha was asking for some help.

Contemporary interpretations of this passage assist us at looking more deeply into the role of women in Jesus' public life. In the past, the story of Martha and Mary has been interpreted as symbolizing the value of contemplative religious life as exemplified by Mary contrasted with active religious life as demonstrated by Martha. The intention seems to have been to indicate that the contemplative life of ever-deepening prayer and union with God was superior to the active life which, although it included prayer, was primarily concerned with taking care of the "busyness" of the world.

In recent years another interpretation has emerged from this story. The newer interpretation stresses that contemplative life and active life are interdependent. One feeds and nourishes the other. Through contemplation we are moved to go out to others in service. The result of serving those in need brings us back to conversation with God for strength and support. Both are essential for discipleship.

Mary had seated herself at the Lord's feet and listened to his words. When Martha complained, "Lord, do you not care that my sister has left me by myself to do the serving? Tell her to help me,"

Jesus' response is inclusive. He does not exclude Martha from doing what Mary is enjoying, nor does he tell Mary to leave him and help her sister. Rather, he invites Martha by telling her that she is "anxious and worried about many things. There is need of only one thing. Mary has chosen the better part and it will not be taken from her."

Jesus implies that neither woman is bound to housework and domestic tasks. He invites both of them to learn from him, to sit with him — the teacher, the rabbi — and to hear his words. He invites them to share the Good News just as the men in his entourage do. Mary seems to have recognized that she was not restricted from sitting with Jesus and communicating with him even though she was a woman. She was his disciple, his follower, learning from him, choosing the better portion.

Martha exhibits some of the lack of self-confidence often found in women who have been indoctrinated with the belief that they are second-class citizens. She failed to take the initiative to assume her full dignity as person. Jesus includes everyone in his mission of love. The more we read Scripture, the more we know that Jesus was not bound by a stereotyped definition of what a woman's role should be. He believed women, too, could be disciples to others, as we shall see more fully in later texts to be discussed. He respected the personhood of women as well as of men.

In all his instructions Jesus taught his disciples what it would cost to be his followers. Jesus, the teacher, was an enabler, as teachers should be. In this situation he enabled his listeners to experience creative thinking by building on his words. Jesus was also chipping away at the cultural repression of women's intellectual abilities. He was truly ahead of his time as he showed that women, as well as men, could enjoy a greater share of the fullness of life, the joy of learning, the excitement of contributing creative thinking to the betterment of society.

The task of contemporary disciples of Christ is clear: we are to cry out his message to all the world, to enable the human person to discover the fullness of what it means to be created in the image, after the likeness, of God.

When we read the Gospel stories it is important for us to question the role of the disciple as it unfolds in the context of the Good News. We need to discover whether our thinking is consistent with the teaching of Jesus. He gives us the true sign of holiness in the story of Mary and Martha — the better portion is to listen to what the Lord is saying, to hear his teaching, and to allow the Spirit of God to transform our lives.

In this scene Mary is doing just that. She is doing what Mary of Nazareth did — pondering all these things. And we? Are we willing to curtail some of our many activities to sit and listen to the Lord speak in our hearts? Sometimes we have difficult questions to ask ourselves if we are to be true disciples of Jesus.

As we reflect on this brief scene we discover more of what is entailed in being disciples of Jesus. We must listen to his teaching. Are we more inclined in our prayer to do all the talking and to allow Jesus only to listen? This story indicates that the better portion is to listen to the words the Lord is speaking. This means that we must relinquish some things, even those done for the good of others, to simply sit at the feet of Jesus and listen to him. It can be difficult to recognize the power of prayer as being greater than all the things we might do. We need to learn that greater things will be accomplished by the disciple who gives time to listen to what Jesus says.

2
Entering the House
Peter's Mother-in-law

Matthew, Mark, and Luke all give an account of the healing of Peter's mother-in-law. Here are the texts of the three accounts.

> Jesus entered the house of Peter, and saw his mother-in-law lying in bed with a fever. He touched her hand, the fever left her, and she rose and waited on him (Matthew 8:14-15).

> On leaving the synagogue he entered the house of Simon and Andrew with James and John. Simon's mother-in-law lay sick with a fever. They immediately told him about her. He approached, grasped her hand, and helped her up. Then the fever left her and she waited on them (Mark 1:29-31).

> After he left the synagogue, he entered the house of Simon. Simon's mother-in-law was afflicted with a severe fever, and they interceded with him about her. He stood over her, rebuked the fever, and it left her. She got up immediately and waited on them (Luke 4:38-39).

There is some slight divergence of wording in each of the narratives, but the theme is the same — primarily, servanthood.

In all three Gospels the healing of Peter's mother-in-law is preceded by other healings. In Matthew, Jesus had just healed the centurion's servant. In both Mark and Luke, Jesus was teaching in the synagogue when he was accosted by a demoniac. He rebuked the unclean spirit, then left the synagogue.

In each account of the healing of Peter's mother-in-law, Jesus entered the house. For this reason the scene is called just that: Entering the House. One of the first notable things in these three accounts is the almost immediate bonding between Jesus and his first four apostles. Further on in the Gospels, the fact that Jesus enters the house has a certain significance. In the course of the narratives when Jesus enters the house with his apostles he often uses this as a time to teach. Sometimes he teaches by words; at other times he teaches by actions.

In this first encounter of Jesus with a woman during his public life (other than, perhaps, with his mother at Cana) he teaches the action of healing. The message to us is that, like him, his followers are to be healers. Matthew does not tell whether the apostles said anything to Jesus about Peter's mother-in-law being ill, but both Mark and Luke indicate that the apostles told Jesus of the woman's infirmity.

What kinds of thoughts might have raced through the mind of Simon's mother-in-law when these five men walked into the house? Did she, for example, think, "Oh, what is Simon thinking of? Here I am sick, too sick to prepare a meal for them, and he brings a guest! There's no one else to take care of things."

Or did she think, "I recognize that man with Simon. He's the one people are coming from all over to listen to. I wonder how Simon persuaded him to come here for a meal. I wish I could get up and wait on them, but I'm just too sick to move."

Of course we don't know what she thought, nor can we, but she becomes a more believable person when we try to enter into her self-talk. All people have their own self-talk. It helps us identify with others when we try to enter into their way of talking to themselves.

Matthew says, "He touched her hand," and Mark tells us that "He . . . grasped her hand, and helped her up." For Luke, Christ's presence was sufficient — "He stood over her, rebuked the fever, and it left her."

The presence of Jesus and his touch in our lives is a healing presence, a healing touch. We can see the compassion that is implicit in the healing process. Jesus took from her a suffering he could remove. He was not deterred by any notion that she was unworthy of his touch upon her life. No, this woman was the object of his attention, the recipient of his healing power. This incident shows that no one is beyond our concern and care.

Jesus walked over to the woman and took her by the hand. How did it feel to her? What was it like to sense the newness of health that permeated her body as he took her hand? Did she experience the surge of good health that causes us to love the living of every day? This healing was not gradual; it happened immediately. All three Evangelists tell us that the woman got up *at once* and began to wait on him/them.

What are the ways Jesus takes us by the hand in our lives? How often are we alert to the touch of his hand upon us, the help he offers, the strength he pours into us? We might also ask how ready are we to welcome Jesus when he enters *our* homes either indirectly through other persons or events or directly through his sacramental presence.

Peter's mother-in-law was accepting and receptive. She allowed Jesus to work the wonder of healing in her life. Sometimes it is difficult for us to receive God's gracious goodness. Does this sound strange? There are times when putting up barriers to the power of Jesus' healing influence is easier than allowing his presence in our lives. Denial can result in no action; acceptance means involvement. A disciple is open to God's action, no matter what the circumstances may be, no matter what involvement may be entailed.

There are other healings of women, as well as of men, in the Gospels. In every healing Jesus gives of himself. Whenever he touches a life, the person is transformed, changed, made new. Only those who are resistant to his touch, who refuse to allow him to work his way with them, fail to be healed. He does nothing against our willingness to accept. He never forces himself on us. We can choose to welcome the Lord into our lives, to allow him to touch us, to transform us, to make us his followers, his disciples. We can also choose not to.

It is important that the response of the woman to Christ's healing was immediate. She responded by an action of servanthood characteristic of discipleship. We can only imagine what might have been the joy with which she moved about as she prepared a meal for these men because she was renewed in body and refreshed in spirit. Jesus had touched and healed her.

From this scene we recognize that we disciples of Jesus strive to be receptive, accepting, healing, compassionate, but most of all we strive to be servants of all. We allow Christ to enter the house of our lives.

3
Is She Dead or Alive?
Jairus' Daughter

In the stories about Jesus' first raising of a dead person, all three writers of the Synoptic Gospels employ the same literary technique of inserting a story within a story. As a result, the citations for each passage below show that a number of verses have been skipped here. (Those verses contain the story of Jesus healing a woman afflicted by hemorrhages and will be dealt with in this book's next scene.)

> While he was saying these things to them, an official came forward, knelt down before him, and said, "My daughter has just died. But come, lay your hand on her, and she will live." Jesus rose and followed him, and so did his disciples. . . .
> When Jesus arrived at the official's house and saw the flute players and the crowd who were making a commotion, he said, "Go away! The girl is not dead but sleeping." And they ridiculed him. When the crowd was put out, he came and took her by the hand, and the little girl arose. And news of this spread throughout all that land (Matthew 9:18-19; 23-26).

When Jesus had crossed again [in the boat] to the other side, a large crowd gathered around him, and he stayed close to the sea. One of the synagogue officials, named Jairus, came forward. Seeing him he fell at his feet and pleaded earnestly with him, saying, "My daughter is at the point of death. Please, come lay your hands on her that she may get well and live." He went off with him, and a large crowd followed and pressed upon him. . . .

While he was still speaking, people from the synagogue official's house arrived and said, "Your daughter has died; why trouble the teacher any longer?" Disregarding the message that was reported, Jesus said to the synagogue official: "Do not be afraid; just have faith." He did not allow anyone to accompany him inside except Peter, James, and John, the brother of James. When they arrived at the house of the synagogue official, he caught sight of a commotion, people weeping and wailing loudly. So he went in and said to them, "Why this commotion and weeping? The child is not dead but asleep." And they ridiculed him. Then he put them all out. He took along the child's father and mother and those who were with him and entered the room where the child was. He took the child by the hand and said to her, *"Talitha koum,"* which means, "Little girl, I say to you, arise!" The girl, a child of twelve, arose immediately and walked around. [At that] they were utterly astounded. He gave strict orders that no one should know this and said that she should be given something to eat (Mark 5:21-24;35-43).

When Jesus returned, the crowd welcomed him, for they were all waiting for him. And a man named Jairus, an official of the synagogue, came forward. He fell at the feet of Jesus and begged him to come to his house, because he had an only daughter, about twelve years old, and she was dying. As he went, the crowds almost crushed him. . . .

While he was still speaking, someone from the synagogue official's house arrived and said, "Your daughter is dead; do not trouble the teacher any longer." On hearing this, Jesus answered him, "Do not be afraid; just have faith and she will be saved." When he arrived at the house he allowed no one to enter with him except Peter and John and James, and the child's father and mother. All were weeping and mourning for her, when he said, "Do not weep any longer, for she is not dead, but sleeping." And they ridiculed him, because they knew that she was dead. But he took her by the hand and called to her, "Child, arise!" Her breath returned and she immediately arose. He then directed that she should be given something to eat. Her parents were astounded, and he instructed them to tell no one what had happened (Luke 8:40-42;49-56).

The theme in this narrative is again one of discipleship. It shows the power of prayer and the importance of trust in Jesus once we have told him our needs. Although the healing of the daughter of Jairus may seem to simply illustrate how Jesus responded to the request of a man of faith, it also shows us that each individual person has immense worth, even a largely unknown girl. In our society life is often devalued. Abortion statistics show how human life is disregarded. In addition, we find other ways of dealing both literal and figurative deathblows to ourselves and others when we create more bombs than are needed and continue practices which discriminate against the elderly, the poor, women, Blacks, people with disabilities, and many more.

To put this narrative in perspective, we turn back to what had preceded the encounter of Jesus and Jairus. Jesus had returned from the land of the Gerasenes. There is a slight deviation in Matthew's account from that of Mark and Luke. In Matthew's Gospel, Jesus had returned from the land of the Gerasenes, had cured a paralytic, and had called the tax collector, Matthew, to be his follower. He then sat down to dinner with a number of tax collectors and sinners, much to the annoyance of the Pharisees who were present. After that, John the Baptizer's disciples came to question him. While he was speaking with them, a synagogue leader came up and approached him.

In both Mark and Luke, when Jesus had crossed back to the other side of the lake from the land of the Gerasenes, he was met by a large crowd. At that time Jairus, an official of the synagogue, came to him for help. We can visualize Jesus being the center of attention for the people.

In this instance Jesus was not just the center of attention for the crowd; he was the one person to whom the leader of the synagogue came to speak. Jairus trusted in his heart that Jesus was the only person who could help. Matthew tells us that Jairus' daughter had just died, but Mark and Luke indicate that she was critically ill and that there was no hope of recovery. They also gave her age — she was a girl of twelve.

When he was asked to help, Jesus responded immediately. There was no hesitancy on his part. Matthew tells us that Jesus stood up and followed the synagogue leader while Mark, having indicated that Jesus was the center of a large crowd, said that the two went off together and a large crowd followed, pushing against Jesus. Luke says that the chief of the synagogue was still speaking when a man came to announce that the girl was dead, then added, "Why bother the teacher further?" Mark's account is similar. People from the official's house arrived to report that the daughter was dead and they, too, asked, "Why bother the teacher further?"

These questions are a necessary part of the story, as we will see. You know, we might have been tempted to say the same thing as the people from the house of the leader of the synagogue. In the face of death there is no help; why bother the teacher? But for Jesus there was more he could and would do. He had already cured the sick; now he would raise the dead to life. The girl was now dead. As we can infer from Jesus' action, none of his believers are inferior. All have a part in his work of redemption, his saving gift of life.

Both Mark and Luke give us Jesus' response to the lack of confidence displayed by the messengers. "Fear is useless," he said. "What is needed is trust." That sounds simple, doesn't it? We might even say to another who is troubled about something in the living of daily life, "Don't worry. Just trust in the Lord."

In reality, however, aren't we afflicted with a certain spiritual illness that we might phrase as fear of trust? Have you ever discovered that it is easy to trust in the Lord as long as you are in charge? Real trust demands abandonment of our control of whatever the situation may be. It demands that we truly put our trust in the Lord.

"Oh, but that's so hard!" we may cry.

In each of the narratives Jesus is ridiculed when he says, "The child is not dead. She is asleep." He allowed only the child's father and mother and his own companions to enter the room with him. In all three accounts Jesus is said to have taken the little girl by the hand. Again we have evidence of the power of his touch on our lives through the example of the touch of his hand first to heal a sick woman and now to raise to new life a little girl who was dead.

Notice, however, that his care did not end with renewal of life for the girl. He went further. He told the parents to give her something to eat, but also cautioned those who were with him not to tell anyone what had happened.

How many of us are spiritually asleep, in need of having Jesus take us by the hand and tell us to "Get up!" Do we feel his touch in our lives and hear his voice in our hearts? We, too, are in need of nourishment — food of the spirit. The disciple is to heal and to nourish and in the act of nourishment to lead the one who is being fed by spiritual food to new life, to transformed life.

In this story of the raising of the daughter of Jairus, it is possible for us to see a foreshadowing of two incredible events that will happen in Jesus' own life — the splendor of Christ's Resurrection and the gift of the Eucharist as nourishment.

The faith of the father brings life to his daughter through his love of her and his trust in Jesus. Yes, *love* and *trust* are the key words. The synagogue leader had total trust in Jesus when he said, "Please come and lay your hand on her and she will come back to life."

Another meaning can be derived from this narrative. When a person offers prayer to Jesus, the now divine lover, that same Jesus brings life. Our maleness or femaleness is not essential; life is. The human spirit is valued for its personhood.

From this scene we understand that we disciples of Jesus, through our faith in him, have the opportunity to raise to new life those who hunger for spiritual nourishment. More than that, the disciples realize the power of prayer. They do not neglect to call on God for the needs of others as well as for the needs of self. The prayer of the synagogue leader brought new life to his daughter. They continue to pray as disciples of Christ, and their prayers have a power we cannot even imagine. By their prayer they bring Christ to those who need his healing presence. Christ will never refuse to respond. We may not understand the manner of his response, but we trust him and we know he will help all who are in need.

One final note for those of us who are disciples of Jesus: through this account Jesus informs us that although he knows our needs he wants us to go to him for help, to put all our trust in him. He tells us quite simply to be like a little child who trusts in a loving parent.

4
The Foolish and the Wise
The Parable of the Ten Bridesmaids

The Synoptic Gospels include three parables dealing with women. Only Matthew gives us the parable of the ten bridesmaids who went out to welcome the groom.

> Then the kingdom of heaven will be like ten virgins who took their lamps and went out to meet the bridegroom. Five of them were foolish and five were wise. The foolish ones, when taking their lamps, brought no oil with them, but the wise brought flasks of oil with their lamps. Since the bridegroom was long delayed, they all became drowsy and fell asleep. At midnight, there was a cry, "Behold, the bridegroom! Come out to meet him!" Then all those virgins got up and trimmed their lamps. The foolish ones said to the wise, "Give us some of your oil, for our lamps are going out." But the wise ones replied, "No, for there may not be enough for us and you. Go instead to the merchants and buy some for yourselves." While they went off to buy it, the bridegroom came and those who were ready went into the wedding feast with him. Then the door was locked. Afterwards, the other virgins came and said, "Lord, Lord, open the door for us!"

But he said in reply, "Amen, I say to you, I do not know you." Therefore, stay awake, for you know neither the day nor the hour (Matthew 25:1-13).

Just prior to telling this parable Jesus has been speaking of the need for preparedness. He has stated in Matthew 24:36 that no one knows the exact day or hour of the coming of the Son of Man. Jesus uses the Parable of the Ten Bridesmaids to bring home to his disciples the importance of his teaching.

We can read "bridegroom" to be "Jesus" and "bride" to be "Church." Everyone receives an invitation to join together in praise of God and to enjoy the happiness of union with him. The ten bridesmaids set an example of what our spiritual destiny will be, depending on whether we are wise or foolish. The parable obviously relates to the uncertainty of time — of the need to be prepared for what will be the end of time for each of us, as well as the uncertainty of the time of the Parousia (the Second Coming). Jesus is teaching not just a lesson of preparedness but also one of fidelity. One who is faithful to God does not need to fear, despite the uncertainty of time. Again and again in the Gospels Jesus emphasizes the blessedness of doing the will of God.

There is no problem of lack of preparedness if one is a true disciple of the Lord. The disciple is servant of all but most particularly servant of the Lord. A servant is ready to do the will of the master even if it goes against the self. Readiness, then, is a characteristic of the servant-disciple.

Readiness was not a characteristic of the foolish bridesmaids. They were unprepared to go to the wedding feast. We can read much into the words "The foolish ones, when taking their lamps, brought no oil with them, but the wise brought flasks of oil with their lamps." The lamps can be interpreted to signify the good deeds of a person's life.

The response of the sensible bridesmaids can seem callous. But there is no way that the sensible ones could give away what they needed. The oil they had symbolizes their service to God. This brings into focus again the importance of recognizing God's will for us and of doing what we can to live according to it. We have seen how Mary of Nazareth did the will of God. Throughout his public life Jesus reiterates the importance of fidelity to God's will. There can be no greater preparedness than this when our "groom" arrives.

Some might counter that the sensible bridesmaids failed their sisters by refusing to give of the oil in their lamps. If we have been blessed by the awareness of God's presence in our lives, there is an urgency within us that moves us to share this gift. We cannot give to another, however, what has already been given to God; but we can share with all those who will receive them the benefits of the graces we have received from the Lord.

Not everyone is willing, however, to accept what is offered at a particular time. Then, when it is too late, they want to have what now is not available. How late is too late for us to give to another? It is never too late to try to hold others in prayer, asking the Lord to fill their lives with love; but we can never force another to accept a gift offered. Our consolation is the realization that God is the final reconciler.

Whether we think of preparedness as relating to the uncertainty of time or as relating to accepting God's gift of himself, this parable focuses on the necessity of taking into account the many uncertainties of life and of being ready to accept what comes to us from the Lord.

We take for ourselves the lessons that apply to us as disciples. Are we ready for the Lord to enter our hearts? Can we accept the immensity of God's love, or are our hearts too full of self for us to make space available? Are we ready at any time for that final call of Jesus to "Come, follow me"? Are we willing to share our spiritual and material possessions with others who have foolishly failed to listen to the quiet call of the Lord?

One thing we know with certainty is that none of us wants to face the closed door blocking us from final union with God. A parable like this one can bring into focus the necessity for the disciple to hear the word of the Lord, to listen to his teaching. "Those who were ready went into the wedding feast with him." Not only do we strive to live in a state of readiness to do God's will, but as disciples of Jesus we seek to help others on their journey to God.

5
"Who Touched Me?"
A Woman With a Hemorrhage

In this reflection we meet a woman who had suffered for twelve years with a hemorrhage. In her actions and in the effect of Jesus upon her life we discover further characteristics of the Christ who came that we might have life and have it more abundantly. This particular scene interrupts the narrative of the raising to life of Jairus' daughter.

> A woman suffering hemorrhages for twelve years came up behind him and touched the tassel on his cloak. She said to herself, "If only I can touch his cloak, I shall be cured." Jesus turned around and saw her, and said, "Courage, daughter! Your faith has saved you." And from that hour the woman was cured (Matthew 9:20-22).

> There was a woman afflicted with hemorrhages for twelve years. She had suffered greatly at the hands of many doctors and had spent all that she had. Yet she was not helped but only grew worse. She had heard about Jesus and came up behind him in the crowd and touched his cloak. She said, "If I but touch his clothes, I shall be cured." Immediately her flow of

blood dried up. She felt in her body that she was healed of her affliction. Jesus, aware at once that power had gone from him, turned around in the crowd and asked, "Who has touched my clothes?" But his disciples said to him, "You see how the crowd is pressing upon you, and yet you ask, 'Who touched me?'" And he looked around to see who had done it. The woman, realizing what had happened to her, approached in fear and trembling. She fell down before Jesus and told him the whole truth. He said to her, "Daughter, your faith has saved you. Go in peace and be cured of your affliction" (Mark 5:25-34).

And a woman afflicted with hemorrhages for twelve years, who [had spent her whole livelihood on doctors and] was unable to be cured by anyone, came up behind him and touched the tassel on his cloak. Immediately her bleeding stopped. Jesus then asked, "Who touched me?" While all were denying it, Peter said, "Master, the crowds are pushing and pressing in upon you." But Jesus said, "Someone has touched me; for I know that power has gone out from me." When the woman realized that she had not escaped notice, she came forward trembling. Falling down before him, she explained in the presence of all the people why she had touched him and how she had been healed immediately. He said to her, "Daughter, your faith has saved you; go in peace" (Luke 8:43-48).

If we want to take the best picture of this scene, a picture that will show on the screen of our minds, we will take Mark's narration and visualize the scene. We see a woman, a poor anonymous woman who carried her pain deep within her. We know something about this woman. What do we know? Mark tells us that she had suffered from hemorrhages for twelve years; that she had received treatment at the hands of doctors of every sort; that she had exhausted her savings in the process; that the affliction was incurable at any doctor's hands; that even though she had gone to doctors of every sort, she got no relief. On the contrary, she only grew worse.

Since she had exhausted her savings, we presume that she must have been poor. She was probably alone, too, because according to Mosaic law the woman would have been considered "unclean" and unfit for contact with other people because of her condition. In today's language, the woman would most likely have had some sort of intestinal or uterine cancer.

Mark and Matthew tell us some of her thoughts as she moved toward Jesus. That she was ill is the essential element of her approach to Jesus to touch his garment. We know something else about this woman — even though she was ill she was also confident, confident that Jesus not only could but *would* heal her. "If I can only touch his cloak, or clothing, or the tassel of his cloak," she thought, "I shall get well."

As we read the three Scripture accounts we are aware of the depth of faith this woman had in the healing power of Jesus, in the power of his presence, in the strength she would gain from simply touching his garment. The crowd gathered closely around Jesus, but the woman moved in close enough to touch him.

We know also that she was a woman of courage. Although we might regard this story as a healing miracle, its significance goes deeper than that. The woman receives more than physical healing; her cure is also an example of sublime faith. It is a story of great courage — the courage of a woman who dared to touch the clothing of a man in public. In Jesus' time disease was regarded as a punishment for sin (see Psalm 38:6-17 and 2 Maccabees 7:37). By seeking healing of her sin she was, in effect, showing her courage that it mattered not at all to her if others saw her as a sinner. She was a woman who had faith in Jesus. The woman had heard about Jesus and saw him as one who was merciful and compassionate: one who had power to heal and who would use this power for her good. She thought she would not be noticed, but in fact she did not escape his awareness of her touch upon his garment.

"Who has touched my clothes?" Jesus asks in this scene. If we had been one of the disciples present at the time we, too, would probably have said "You can see how there are a bunch of people here crowding us in. How can you ask, 'Who touched me?' " The disciples must have wondered why he made a fuss about it, why he asked who had touched him when so many were bumping against him.

Jesus' motive was more than pragmatic; it was intended to teach a lesson of the spirit, the power of faith. We all know how we can sometimes feel and do something very courageous one moment and then, after the fact, we feel fear of the unknown welling up within us. Mark tells us that the woman was fearful and beginning to tremble once Jesus demanded to know who had touched him. The courage of the previous moment melted with the questioning. She fell at his feet, Luke said, and before the whole assemblage she explained why she had touched him and how she had been cured instantly.

How hard it must have been for her. How would you have felt announcing to the whole assemblage this story of pain, illness, despair, and finally of hope? Jesus' healing power was her last hope. Greater than the fear that had forced her to confess her action was the reward of telling the world that Jesus is the Christ, that he had made her whole, that simply touching the garment he was wearing was sufficient to heal her when the expertise of doctors had failed.

The sound of Jesus' words, "Daughter, your faith has saved you. Go in peace and be cured of your affliction" must have been beautiful. The gift he bestows on the woman is not only physical strength, it is also spiritual strength. He gives her his own peace, a peace that comes to her through her expression of faith in him. Peace, then, can be recognized as the fruit of faith.

The disciple learns so much from this encounter of Jesus and the sick woman. Just as nothing is beyond the power of Jesus to heal, no affliction is too great to present to him. Just as no person is beneath the concern of the Lord, so is no one beneath the concern of Christ's followers. The poor, the alienated, the sick, the fearful, the broken, whether physically or spiritually fractured — all are in need of our care. The woman experienced the mercy and compassion of Jesus because her faith was humble, accepting, expectant, and courageous.

How often do we reflect on the occasions in our lives when we have experienced the healing peace of Jesus? Do we need to reflect on this? It was he who promised us, "Peace I leave with you; my peace I give to you" (John 14:27).

On the day that the woman touched Jesus' garment, she knew a gamut of emotions — pain and healing, courage and fear, faith and peace, poverty enriched by the touch of Jesus' love and compassion. What wealth she took with her as she left the scene! What wealth she now had to share with others.

We understand from the narrative of the woman with the hemorrhage that we disciples of Jesus strive not just to heal the sick but also to bring peace to those who suffer. Jesus felt the touch of the woman on his life. He gave of himself to the woman in this cure, allowed her to feel his touch on her life. The disciple, too, understands the need to offer self to others in need.

6
Power of a Mother's Prayer
The Possessed Girl

We have seen Jesus speak to us about the traits of servanthood, of bringing to him those who need his healing presence, of giving of self to those in need. Now we will renew our understanding of the power of a mother's prayer as we consider the narrative of the Canaanite woman.

Read and search for traits the disciple needs in order to serve the cause of Jesus — to continue his mission in our own time.

> Then Jesus went from that place and withdrew to the region of Tyre and Sidon. And behold, a Canaanite woman of that district came and called out, "Have pity on me, Lord, Son of David! My daughter is tormented by a demon." But he did not say a word in answer to her. His disciples came and asked him. "Send her away, for she keeps calling out after us." He said in reply, "I was sent only to the lost sheep of the house of Israel." But the woman came and did him homage, saying, "Lord, help me." He said in reply, "It is not right to take the food of the children and throw it to the dogs." She said, "Please, Lord, for even the dogs eat the scraps that fall from the table of their masters." Then Jesus said to her in reply, "O woman, great is your faith! Let it be done for you as you

wish." And her daughter was healed from that hour (Matthew 15:21-28).

From that place he went off to the district of Tyre. He entered a house and wanted no one to know about it, but he could not escape notice. Soon a woman whose daughter had an unclean spirit heard about him. She came and fell at his feet. The woman was a Greek, a Syrophoenician by birth, and she begged him to drive the demon out of her daughter. He said to her, "Let the children be fed first. For it is not right to take the food of the children and throw it to the dogs." She replied and said to him, "Lord, even the dogs under the table eat the children's scraps." Then he said to her, "For saying this, you may go. The demon has gone out of your daughter." When the woman went home, she found the child lying in bed and the demon gone (Mark 7:24-30).

This account bears a great similarity to the story of the woman who suffered from a hemorrhage in that it is a pronouncement on faith. Faith in Jesus results in healing.

Both Matthew and Mark indicate that Jesus went to a new place of ministry, to the district of Tyre and Sidon. He went into Gentile territory, perhaps because he did not want to be recognized, as Mark says. Yet he could not escape notice, much as he seemed to desire some quiet for himself. A Canaanite woman, Matthew says, presented herself to him. Mark identifies the woman as a Greek, "a Syrophoenician by birth." Mark seems more emphatic than Matthew about her being Gentile both by religion and by birth. That, however, did not deter her from asking pity from Jesus. She, too, had a mission, one that was most important to her. The intensity of her desire to help her child gave her the courage to be bold enough to ask this Jew for help. She knew he could do for her what she asked.

All of us, I feel sure, understand something of the close bond that exists between mother and child. This bond is evident in the narrative we are considering. This Gentile woman, this Canaanite, cried out to Jesus, "Lord, Son of David, have pity on me! My daughter is terribly troubled by a demon."

Jesus seemingly ignored her. He gave her no word of response, Matthew says. Of all types of treatment that cause pain to a person, none carries hurt like that of being ignored. Yet the woman persisted. Love for her child gave strength to her.

The disciples wanted Jesus to "get rid of her." They said to him, "She keeps calling after us." Of course Jesus was well aware of this, and perhaps he wanted his disciples to see for themselves that she was persistent in asking help from him.

Jesus finally acknowledged her presence and replied, "it is not right to take the food of the children and throw it to the dogs." To derive the deeper meaning of this story we need to understand that "the children" symbolize the Jews. Gentiles, at that time and in that part of the world, were commonly called "dogs."

Matthew tells us that Jesus told her his mission was only to the lost sheep of the house of Israel. Oddly enough, however, he was in Gentile territory. We might wonder why he went there if the Gentiles were not included in his mission. This leads us to an understanding that the presence of Jesus in Gentile territory is an instance of the universalism of Jesus' concern and care for all people, no matter where they were or would be throughout the world. He does not deny salvation to the Gentiles, because he says: "Let the children of the household satisfy themselves at table first," indicating that after the sons and daughters had had their fill, others, too, would find that there was enough to eat.

It is also interesting to us to note that the "children" and the "dogs," as they were called, are in the same house, eating in the same room. Jesus is not refusing to feed these "dogs" but they must wait until after the children have had the opportunity to enjoy the meal to its fullness. Then the pups may be fed.

The Canaanite woman exhibits remarkable logic when she points out that "even the dogs under the table eat the children's scraps." That was the clinching argument. Jesus had enabled the woman to prove her faith in him.

"O woman," he said, "great is your faith! Let it be done for you as you wish." Matthew says that was the moment the demon left her daughter. Mark had Jesus himself say, "The demon has gone out of your daughter." This release, this healing, was brought about by the mother's faith and by her persevering prayer.

Was Jesus testing this woman's faith? Was he teaching us a lesson about the power of prayer? Her perseverance is a powerful example for us. The woman's faith in Jesus did not yield to intimidation, threats, or refusal. As Christ's disciples today there are times when we are tempted to give up, to accept that the Lord does not want to answer our prayer, to think that he is not listening. These are difficult times for one who calls on God for help, but they are the very times when it is most important to persist in asking for what we need. We have heard the lesson that we are closest to success when we seem most doomed to failure. The Canaanite woman instinctively seems to understand this.

Does Jesus use the process of calling us to persistent prayer as a way of leading us to develop a deeper trust in him? This way of allowing our faith in him to be put to the test is also a means of leading to the discovery of how strong our faith is. It shows our willingness to avoid the demons of doubt and discouragement.

The scene of the power of a mother's prayer brings us face-to-face with the need for persevering prayer. We are reminded that Jesus does not turn away from anyone who comes to him for help. The lessons for us as Christ's disciples of today are clear — everyone is worthy of our time and attention. All of us need to understand the power of persevering prayer.

7
The Least Is the Most
The Poor Widow

The Gospel account about the poor widow is a very brief episode, indeed. But in this case it becomes obvious that "the least is the most." That is exactly what Jesus tells us in this scene. Although the account is very brief, it is very important.

> When he looked up he saw some wealthy people putting their offerings into the treasury and he noticed a poor widow putting in two small coins. He said, "I tell you truly, this poor widow put in more than all the rest; for those others have all made offerings from their surplus wealth, but she, from her poverty, has offered her whole livelihood" (Luke 21:1-4).

Matthew omits the story of the widow's mite. Mark and Luke place it at the end of Jesus' ministry. The story follows Jesus' condemnation of Jewish leaders "who like to go around in long robes and love greetings in marketplaces, seats of honor in synagogues, and places of honor at banquets" (Luke 20:46).

Once again we see how Jesus relates to a poor, anonymous woman — a widow who has little to support herself but to whom

Yahweh is all-important. We can envision Jesus as he sits opposite the treasury, see him as he observes people putting money into the collection box. He does not condemn the wealthy who put in sizable amounts. They are doing right in making a contribution to the support of God's house. But Jesus praises the widow who put in far less money than the wealthy did. We know nothing else about her, yet her very action caused Jesus to admire her. She vanishes from our sight, but Jesus does not let her example escape our consideration.

The widow exemplified the biblical meaning of sacrifice. We are accustomed to thinking of sacrifice as "giving up." The biblical meaning of sacrifice is "giving to." We give to the one we love because of that love. Naturally we give the best of what we have because sacrifice is a gift of love to one we love. The woman was giving to God out of love, not out of poverty.

Strange, isn't it, that we can be poor and rich at the same time? This story illustrates that truth. The woman was poor in the goods of this world, but she was rich in her love of God.

Although this is a short text, much can be read into it. In a sense the woman was laying down her life for love of God's house which is love for God himself. Soon Jesus would be laying down his life for love of God and for us, the people of God. Could this event be a foreshadowing of the gift of his life that Jesus would soon make for us?

We contemporary disciples give to others after the example of Jesus. The little, insignificant gift we think we have might be witness enough to enable another to have faith in God, to trust in his mercy and compassion. We can never underestimate the importance of example.

At the same time, we disciples are never poor, never destitute. One who loves and follows the Lord is endowed with the riches of a graced life — the grace of the presence of the Lord himself. What greater wealth could we want or imagine than that of being loved by him whose love brought him to the complete giving of his life for us?

The actual money is not the center of the story. In fact, it is of least importance. The story challenges us to follow the one who gave all for us. What can we give in return? What love, compassion, forbearance, and sensitivity? Jesus shows us the way through the example of this poor widow and through the example of his own gift of life.

From this brief scene the contemporary disciple learns about the beauty of our personal gifts. It is not what we give that is of greatest importance. What is important is the love that prompts the giving. The disciple is one who gives out of love.

8
The Search
The Parable of the Woman and the Lost Coin

This parable is one of three consecutive ones in which Luke recounts the theme of divine love and forgiveness. The first is the parable of the lost sheep; the second, the lost coin; and the third, the prodigal son. In the story of the lost coin, Jesus uses a woman as the story's main character:

> Or what woman having ten coins and losing one would not light a lamp and sweep the house, searching carefully until she finds it? And when she does find it, she calls together her friends and neighbors and says to them, "Rejoice with me because I have found the coin that I lost." In just the same way, I tell you, there will be rejoicing among the angels of God over one sinner who repents (Luke 15:8-10).

Luke's writing is quite visual. In this instance we can empathize with the woman. A woman with only ten silver pieces is probably poor. When she has lost one she increases her poverty so she searches for what is lost. The woman did not live in a throw-away society like ours. We can almost feel her sense of panic.

She finds her broom that is probably made of rushes to sweep the dirt floor. The room has only a single opening at the door. We see her stop to light a lamp, an action that is costly, but the coin is of greater worth than the cost of the oil for the lamp. As she sweeps she listens, trying to hear the sound or tinkle of the coin against the floor. We see her search in the dim light looking for the lost piece of silver.

One lost coin seems so little a sum to go to such work to find. But the one coin that is lost, like the lost sheep, is essential for completeness, for fullness, for wholeness. Something is lacking when even one is lost. The woman is searching for the totality of what she had had. She wants the fullness of her treasure.

This short parable implies many things. All of us can think of our own lack of completeness, wholeness, and holiness. If even one person is in need, we do not experience completeness. If one person suffers, we must look to find a way to alleviate that suffering. If another rejoices, unless that person has someone with whom to rejoice, there is an emptiness despite seeming fullness.

When the woman found the silver piece, she called her friends and neighbors to rejoice with her. In the news there was once a story about a man who had never had a birthday party. One day he had enough money to celebrate his birth, and he decided to have a party. There was one problem; he had no friends. What did he do? He kidnapped people to celebrate with him. This extreme example speaks of our need for community. We want to celebrate the good things that happen in life. We need community.

Jesus tells us that "there will be rejoicing among the angels of God over one sinner who repents." Can you recall the sense of joy you felt when you first experienced reconciliation with a friend, family member, or with God? When such a thing happens we find a peace of soul that has been lost. There is a freeing sensation. We understand once again the meaning of wholeness, of completeness. One thing that had been missing made the difference. Now it has been recovered. This short parable has meaning for all of us.

The woman recognized her poverty, her lack, and she was aware of her need to search for what was lost. Do we identify our poverties? Do we recognize in ourselves any lack of spiritual completeness? If so, do we search for what is lost?

As disciples of Jesus we have great responsibilities and opportunities, as suggested by this parable. Many persons have lost the way to God. We question how we can light the lamp of God's presence in us and in those who are unaware of that presence within. As God's disciples we are partners with the Lord who searches for the lost ones. It is not necessary for us to see results, but rather that we persevere in prayer for those who are in need, whatever the need may be.

We rejoice with and for them when they have recovered wholeness. We understand more fully that there will be the same kind of joy before the angels of God over one repentant sinner. To repent is to turn to God, to be reconciled, to be at one with, to experience the peace that the world cannot give.

The responsibility of the disciple is great. Many there are who have lost touch with God in their lives and are unaware of their loss. The things of the world can never fill the emptiness they experience, but they seem not to recognize this. When we reflect on discipleship we realize that we have a responsibility to those who enjoy fewer spiritual blessings than we, even though this lack may be due to their own failure. But we cannot allow their failure to become our failure. We must search for them and seek to help them.

At the same time we must be alert to our own needs. Our focus is not only on others; it must also be on ourself — on our inner life. Each day we need to be conscious of any problems in our spiritual growth and to rejoice in the gains that the Spirit of God enables in us.

The responsibility of the disciple is great — the rejoicing when the lost has been found is beyond description.

9
Women Are Disciples, Too
Mary Magdalene, Joanna, Susanna

Only three verses are necessary to communicate to the world what the women in this scene did and why they were important. The verses are brief so we must be alert to what we are reading in order to discover the message for us twentieth-century disciples.

> Afterward he journeyed from one town and village to another, preaching and proclaiming the good news of the kingdom of God. Accompanying him were the Twelve and some women who had been cured of evil spirits and infirmities, Mary, called Magdalene, from whom seven demons had gone out, Joanna, the wife of Herod's steward Chuza, Susanna, and many others who provided for them out of their resources (Luke 8:1-3).

Only Luke specifically identifies the women who served Jesus in this particular way. Indeed, Luke mentions women more often than the other Gospels do; thus some commentators have called Luke's Gospel the ''Gospel of Women.''

Jesus disregarded Jewish customs of ignoring women in public. Rabbis did not speak to women if they passed them along the street. Some rabbis even doubted the ability of women to learn the Torah. Not so with Jesus. He paid special attention to them both in public and in private.

In this particular instance, Luke shows that Jesus not only offered new dignity to women by permitting them to hear the Good News of the Kingdom of God, but that he even allowed them to participate in his ministry. They and the Twelve were with him as he journeyed to preach in many towns and villages.

We have no idea how many women accompanied Jesus. Luke gives us the names of three, one of them being Mary, called the Magdalene, from whom Jesus had driven seven demons. The concept of seven demons is usually interpreted to signify the seven capital sins of pride, avarice (greed), lust, envy, gluttony, anger, and sloth (laziness). Joanna is identified as the wife of Chuza who was a steward of Herod Antipas. We might wonder why a royal official would allow his wife to minister to Jesus. As for Susanna, we have only her name. But the fact that there were others is indicated by Luke's statement "and many others who provided for them out of their resources."

Obviously these women were also Jesus' disciples because of their direct assistance to him.

The Gospel author does not say who provided the women with income. We do not know how they managed to care not only for themselves but also for Jesus and his special group of followers. We are simply told that these women had been helped by Jesus and they showed their gratitude by helping him and those who accompanied him.

Obviously the women did not discriminate in their service. They did not, for example, say that this one would care for Jesus because he had done something for her but that she would not serve the disciples. From what we read in this short excerpt, the women were considerate of the needs of all the members of the group. All were cared for.

These women's examples help us question our own servanthood. How do I serve Christ in others? Am I interested in the problems of the unemployed, farmers, resident aliens, the poor, the alienated, and so many others? Do we who look at the example of these women do what we can to care for the people around us who are in need? What is demanded of a disciple of Jesus?

Undoubtedly all of us have either experienced serious depression or know of people who have. The problem is so great that in many cases it leads to suicide. What need there is for help! We know the stresses of our society. Sometimes we get so caught up in our own problems that we cannot or *do not* recognize the greater needs of others. One of the ways we can help ourselves is by caring for another.

Have you experienced the joy that comes from helping another or by doing something gentle and caring for another person? It is possible to lose ourselves, to arrest our concentration on our own problems, by seeing the needs of others and by trying to help them. This action takes sensitivity and thoughtfulness on our part. It results in awareness that we have taken to heart Jesus' admonition that whatever we do for another we do for him. That means our actions of love and compassion draw us closer to the desired union with God.

From this brief scene in Luke's Gospel we come to understand that it is as true today as it was in the first century that we look after others. Life with all its complexities and hardships demands that today's disciples of Jesus follow the example of the women who served him and his apostles. There is so much truth to the saying that when we give, we receive. At the same time, serving another is very demanding and often unappreciated. Yet gratitude for what we do for another is not what the disciple is looking for. The follower of Jesus instead strives to become servant of all. Truly, the cost of discipleship is high!

10
Compassionate Love
A Widow and Her Dead Son

Again, this particular scene is found only in Luke. It is the story of the raising to life of the dead son of the widow of Nain.

> Soon afterward he journeyed to a city called Nain, and his disciples and a large crowd accompanied him. As he drew near to the gate of the city, a man who had died was being carried out, the only son of his mother, and she was a widow. A large crowd from the city was with her. When the Lord saw her, he was moved with pity for her and said to her, "Do not weep." He stepped forward and touched the coffin; at this the bearers halted, and he said, "Young man, I tell you, arise!" The dead man sat up and began to speak, and Jesus gave him to his mother. Fear seized them all, and they glorified God, exclaiming, "A great prophet has arisen in our midst," and "God has visited his people." This report about him spread through the whole of Judea and in all the surrounding region (Luke 7:11-17).

In this scene we become aware of much pageantry. We can easily visualize Jesus entering the town of Nain with his disciples and a large crowd. In Luke, more than in any of the other Gospels, Jesus is often surrounded by a large crowd. As they neared the gate of the town, they were met by another group of people — members of a funeral procession. We might well conclude that the sympathy of the townspeople for the widow was great. Her only son was dead. The people of the town were supportive of the widow in this time of her sorrow.

Jesus, too, was moved with pity for the woman. He demonstrates his compassionate love when he goes over to the widow who undoubtedly is a stranger to him. We hear him tell her, "Do not cry." Then he turns from her and touches the coffin. He doesn't seem to say anything to the bearers, but at his touch on the coffin, the bearers stop.

We can enter more fully into the scene if we think of ourselves as part of the funeral throng. We identify with the crowd, and we identify with the widow. We have heard the words of this man, have watched his actions. We are filled with amazement at what we have seen and heard.

Wonder of wonders! The dead man sits up and begins to speak. We experience fear at this incredible miracle. A dead man has been raised to life! Praise God for his goodness to this widow!

We cannot help but experience fear mixed with our wonder. We see this man, this stranger, lead the now risen son to the mother. We are filled with amazement at this compassionate love.

Although Luke is recounting something that happened in the first century, we twentieth-century disciples also learn from the example of love we witness through our reading. When we read Scripture, if we locate ourselves in the scene we are considering, we find that we can respond immediately to the action of the Lord in our lives. He is so very present to us.

We can reflect further on this incident of compassionate love. We might consider some instances today of power over life and death in the spiritual and psychological realms. In so many ways we can "kill" another. By a look, by a word, by ignoring the other we can take life from the person. We sometimes "cut" another dead, as the expression says.

Furthermore, we are aware that some people use their fellow humans as objects rather than recognizing the dignity of the person. True, as we noted earlier, Luke was writing for the people of the first century. But have you noticed — and I'm sure you have — that one of the beauties of Scripture is its relevance to the world of every age?

Rather than thinking of how we can destroy one another, can we consider ways we might raise another to new life? When someone is in pain from the many trials that confront the human person, we can ease the burden of pain by sharing it. Often a suffering man or woman needs someone who is willing to listen to the story of sorrow. After telling the story, the one who has suffered is lifted to new hope for the future. There is something about sharing sorrow that diminishes the pain, as well as something about sharing love that increases joy.

So many ways exist whereby we can raise another to newness of life — with a smile, a word of encouragement, a touch that speaks of love, of caring. We can raise another to new life by being enablers. Too often we fail to recognize gifts or talents. Then a person comes along, stops to visit with us, helps us recognize what seems hidden to our eyes, enables us to develop some talent that had been buried in us, a talent we had not recognized. The one who enables raises the other to new life, to new appreciation of what God has bestowed on us. We can do this for others.

Unless we take the time to turn aside from our own pursuits as Jesus did in this narrative, unless we are moved by pity for one who suffers, one who mourns, one who bears the burden of loneliness, we will not be enablers, we will not put the spark of life into a person dying inside for want of a friend, for someone to care, someone to listen.

This kind of service can be extremely time-consuming. Aren't we all busy people? Do we readily excuse ourselves from responsibility to those in need? Can we be at peace within ourselves if we do this?

Opportunities abound to be of help to others, to raise them to new life. A missed opportunity is a loss of the chance to imitate Jesus, to show compassionate love.

The disciple follows the example of the master. Jesus teaches us by his action toward the anonymous widow. Once again we understand that for Jesus and for the disciple, no one is unimportant. Everyone merits our care, our concern, and our compassionate love.

11
Winning the Case
The Parable of the Widow and the Judge

Folk wisdom tells us "The squeaky wheel gets the grease" to illustrate how we must be persistent if we are to get what we need. Jesus knew this when he told the story of the widow and the unscrupulous judge.

Then he told them a parable about the necessity for them to pray always without becoming weary. He said, "There was a judge in a certain town who neither feared God nor respected any human being. And a widow in that town used to come to him and say, 'Render a just decision for me against my adversary.' For a long time the judge was unwilling, but eventually he thought, 'While it is true that I neither fear God nor respect any human being, because this widow keeps bothering me I shall deliver a just decision for her lest she finally come and strike me.' " The Lord said, "Pay attention to what the dishonest judge says. Will not God then secure the rights of his chosen ones who call out to him day and night? Will he be slow to answer them? I tell you, he will see to it that justice is done for them speedily. But when the

Son of Man comes, will he find faith on earth?'' (Luke 18:1-8).

The parable Jesus tells is about the necessity of continuing prayer and trusting that God listens to prayer. The story is quite short. We enter in the middle of things. The judge does not fear God nor does he respect any human being. The plot revolves around the rights of the woman against her opponent. The judge refused to grant her her rights. Why? Jesus refers to him as a corrupt judge. Most likely he wanted to be paid a bribe for doing what was his rightful work, but the woman didn't have money for a bribe. Nevertheless she prevailed over him. She was persistent in her demand for justice despite the refusal of the judge to rule justly.

We get an insight into the thinking of the judge that explains his reason for finally giving the woman what she wanted. ''While it is true that I neither fear God nor respect any human being, because this widow keeps bothering me I shall deliver a just decision for her lest she finally come and strike me.'' Literally he reasoned that he would do justice to the woman to save himself from losing his mind by her persistent demands for justice. He dealt justice not for justice's sake, but for his own liberation from her demands.

What happened after that does not have to be detailed — such is the beauty of a short story. The woman got what she asked; the judge delivered himself from his oppressor. Then Jesus drew a lesson for all to learn — that justice will come to all who call on God with persevering prayer. The woman put her faith in her persistence. She wore down the barriers the judge had erected against her demands. Can a compassionate God erect barriers to keep us out? Can the Lord refuse to grant us what we need and ask for?

The disciple of Jesus tries to pray always and not lose heart. Do you truly believe in the power of prayer? We are not asking justice from a corrupt judge when we speak to God. We are present to the one who is always present to us, always attentive to us, always listening to what we have to say.

If we do not believe in the power of prayer, then we doubt God's love for us. He will give us swift justice against oppression, Jesus says. Nonetheless, we must understand that God's ways are not our ways, that at times his answer to our prayer is at variance with what we wanted or expected. But we hear again the words of Jesus that we must pray always and not lose heart.

You know, it wouldn't hurt us a bit to reflect on the tactics of the widow in her action against the unjust judge. Can't you just see her coming to him — or coming at him — daily and asking for justice? And do you see him watch her arrival and say, "Oh, no. Not you again." Until finally he is forced to capitulate to her demands to save his own sanity.

Of course we are not dealing with an unjust judge, but we need to learn from the action of the widow to come daily to God to ask for whatever it is we need.

Do you truly believe in the power of prayer? It's one thing to say we do, but quite another not to lose heart. The disciple, like the widow, is persistent. The disciple of Jesus knows that no prayer goes unanswered, even when the answer is "no." But the very action of praying strengthens the one who prays to accept whatever answer comes. The peace of God prevails.

We who are Christ's followers must continue his mission of love with our caring, compassion, and sharing. We must be teachers, enablers, leaders, peacemakers. As we strive to be servants of all, we must provide for the spiritual and material needs of ourselves and others as best we can. Above all we must pray always and not lose heart.

Both the women and the men who follow Christ are to be people of faith, true to his teachings which taught us how to live in a way that is pleasing to God. It isn't always easy, but it isn't always hard. It is, indeed, a challenge. Can we accept this challenge?

12
"Who Let Her In?"
A Sinful Woman

This story of the woman who anoints Jesus' head (or feet depending on which Gospel is used) is also included in the Gospel of John. However, we will continue to deal only with the narratives of Matthew, Mark, and Luke.

Because these readings are lengthy, only the text in Mark's Gospel appears here. This story also appears in Matthew 26:6-13 and Luke 7:36-50.

When he was in Bethany reclining at table in the house of Simon the leper, a woman came with an alabaster jar of perfumed oil, costly genuine spikenard. She broke the alabaster jar and poured it on his head. There were some who were indignant. "Why has there been this waste of perfumed oil? It could have been sold for more than three hundred days' wages and the money given to the poor." They were infuriated with her. Jesus said, "Let her alone. Why do you make trouble for her? She has done a good thing for me. The poor you will always have with you, and whenever you wish you can do good to them, but you will not always have me. She has done what she could. She has anticipated anointing my body for burial. Amen, I say to you, wherever the gospel is proclaimed to the whole world, what she has done will be told in memory of her" (Mark 14:3-9).

Just as in other accounts given by the three Evangelists, there are similarities and differences. Matthew and Mark place the scene in Bethany at the house of Simon the leper. Some scholars think Simon was identified in this way because Jesus had cleansed him of leprosy. That is simply a theory. Luke doesn't identify the host initially but merely speaks of him as a certain Pharisee who invited Jesus to dine with him. Later, after reading the thoughts of the host, Jesus addresses him as Simon.

In each narrative the episode takes place at table. The woman is not mentioned by name. Matthew and Mark speak of her as "a woman" while Luke adds "a sinful woman in the city." Matthew describes her as carrying a jar of costly perfume, but Mark is more specific — the jar of perfume is made from expensive aromatic spikenard. Luke speaks of "a flask of ointment."

Both Matthew and Mark tell us the woman poured the perfume on his head. It was the custom to anoint the head generously at banquets. Mark adds the note "she broke the jar and poured it on his head." This calls to mind another custom of the time. To retain its fragrance, enough perfume for one application was sealed in small alabaster vases. The contents could be used only by breaking the vessel.

Matthew says the disciples grew indignant. Mark indicates that only some at the table reacted, while Luke reports the thoughts of the Pharisee: "If this man were a prophet, he would know who and what sort of woman this is who is touching him, that she is a sinner" (Luke 7:39). Neither of the other two Evangelists we are considering say this about the woman. But we must remember that each is writing for a specific group of persons and therefore emphasizes what he considers important to carry his message. Luke has a further teaching he wants to point out to the Christians he is addressing.

Matthew and Mark — as well as John in his account — indicate the cause of the grumbling and the opposition to the action of the woman was that the perfume could have been sold and the money given to the poor. Isn't it strange that they did not seem to think Jesus was worthy of this mark of respect?

Jesus, however, seemed aware of this lack of sensitivity on the part of his friends. He rebuked them, asking why they criticized the woman for the good deed she had done. Then he added: "The poor you will always have with you, but you will not always have me." He continued by saying, as Mark reports: "She has done what she could. She has anticipated anointing my body for burial. Amen, I say to you, wherever the gospel is proclaimed to the whole world, what she has done will be told in memory of her."

Matthew and Mark interpret the story as showing preparation for Jesus' death, while Luke has it placed earlier in the life of Jesus. That is why Luke's account has a different slant or lesson to it. Jesus read the Pharisee's thoughts and then said, "Simon, I have something to say to you" (Luke 7:40). He tells of two men who owed money to a certain money lender; one owed 500 coins, the other 50. Neither could repay his debt, so the money-lender wrote them off. Then Jesus asked Simon which borrower was more grateful. Simon answered correctly — the one to whom he had remitted the larger sum.

Jesus then turned toward the woman whom Luke had indicated was a known sinner. (And who of us isn't?) Jesus paralleled what Simon had failed to do and what the woman had done for him.

1. Simon gave no water for his feet.
   The woman washed his feet with her tears and wiped them with her hair.

2. Simon gave him no kiss.
   The woman had not ceased kissing his feet since she entered.
3. Simon did not anoint his head with oil.
   The woman anointed Jesus' feet with perfume.

Finally Jesus made his point — her many sins are forgiven because of her great love. He said "The one to whom little is forgiven, loves little" (Luke 7:47). He turned to the woman and said, "Your sins are forgiven. . . . Your faith has saved you; go in peace" (Luke 7:48,50). His fellow guests wondered who this was who even forgives sins.

The role of the woman in the story is one of compassion, of comforting. The disciples allowed reason to rule, and they failed in compassion. They thought only of the money they could have gained by selling the perfume.

The woman was not deterred from her action of love. We who live in the twentieth century seem to think that money is power. Not so for the woman who showed love through her caring ministration. For her, as for all who know and love God, money is not the real measure of power. Love is power. Love was the motive that brought the woman to the house of Simon. Love was not to be contained in an alabaster vase. No, for love to be true to itself it must be poured out. Love can never be contained. It must break out, pour out, be lavished on another, become the fragrance of life, the perfumed oil of peace.

Jesus understood this. He accepted what the woman did for him, for he recognized that compassionate love is as important — more important, indeed — than the rational concern about spending money that could have been used for the poor. He called attention to the truth that the poor would always be part of the human condition. He also noted that he would not be with them always in his human condition.

Jesus was acutely aware of his coming death. In a sense, all of life is preparation for death. Ordinarily we do not consider this. We recognize the inevitability of death, know that someday we will release our hold on life. Indeed, we hope to enjoy the incredible mystery of seeing God, but we do not anticipate this face-to-face reality just yet.

Although reality eludes us, it did not elude Jesus. He knew. He had come up to Jerusalem to face his own death. He knew the hatred he had inspired in the chief priests and elders of the people, but he did not change his tactics. He continued to live as he had lived all during his public life.

We, his disciples, do the same. We know that life is preparation for death, and we continue to live according to this truth. We are not deterred from living life fully, to be fully alive. The disciple also learns from the example of Jesus in this narrative to be gracious in accepting the gesture of compassionate love that is offered by another. We are mindful in his committing the love action of this anonymous woman to perpetual and universal memory when he says, " . . . wherever the gospel is proclaimed to the whole world, what she has done will be told in memory of her."

In this scene we witness a woman in love with her Lord, a woman who shows the world how to care for Christ in daily life, to pour out love on him by pouring out love on others, especially the poor. Discipleship calls us to this.

13
Present to the Beloved
The Women at the Foot of the Cross

Many times we can demonstrate our love by simply being present to the one who suffers. This scene takes place on Calvary. Jesus has died.

> There were many women there, looking on from a distance, who had followed Jesus from Galilee, ministering to him. Among them were Mary Magdalene and Mary the mother of James and Joseph, and the mother of the sons of Zebedee.
>
> When it was evening, there came a rich man from Arimathea named Joseph. . . . He went to Pilate and asked for the body of Jesus; then Pilate ordered it to be handed over. Taking the body, Joseph wrapped it [in] clean linen and laid it in his new tomb that he had hewn in the rock. Then he rolled a huge stone across the entrance to the tomb and departed. But Mary Magdalene and the other Mary remained sitting there, facing the tomb (Matthew 27:55-61).

> There were also women looking on from a distance. Among them were Mary Magdalene, Mary the mother of the younger James and of Joses, and Salome. These women had

followed him when he was in Galilee and ministered to him. There were also many other women who had come up with him to Jerusalem. . . . Mary Magdalene and Mary the mother of Joses watched where he was laid (Mark 15:40-41,47).

All his acquaintances stood at a distance, including the women who had followed him from Galilee and saw these events.

The women who had come from Galilee with him followed behind, and when they had seen the tomb and the way in which his body was laid in it, they returned and prepared spices and perfumed oils. Then they rested on the sabbath according to the commandment (Luke 23:49,55-56).

All three Evangelists identify the women who were present as being those who had followed Jesus from Galilee to minister to his needs. We can only search our own hearts to reflect on the depth of love that matches the depth of sorrow at the loss of one who is loved so dearly. Matthew and Mark identify some of the women — Mary Magdalene, Mary the mother of James and Joseph, the mother of Zebedee's sons. But Mark notes further that "there were many other women who had come up with him to Jerusalem."

Matthew and Luke tell of Joseph, a wealthy man from Arimathea, "who was himself a disciple of Jesus." Joseph requested the body of Jesus from Pilate and the order was given for its release. The writing is truly graphic. With love and reverence, Joseph takes down the body of the Lord, wraps it in fine fresh linen, then lays it in his own new tomb which had been hewn from a formation of rock. No one had yet been buried in the tomb.

Then Matthew says, "he rolled a huge stone across the entrance to the tomb. But Mary Magdalene and the other Mary remained sitting there, facing the tomb." Mark notes that "Mary Magdalene and Mary the mother of Joses watched where he was laid,'' while Luke tells us that ''the women who had come from Galilee with him followed behind, and . . . they had seen the tomb and the way in which his body was laid in it.''

From these three accounts we know there was no question about where Jesus' body had been laid. The women were present and they observed the place. Since this was, as Luke says, ''the day of preparation, and the sabbath was about to begin, they went home to prepare spices and perfumes. They observed the sabbath as a day of rest in accordance with the law.'' This allows for the transition to the final scene.

It is indeed important that the women were so certain of the burial place. They would not be mistaken when they returned after the Sabbath. If there were those who would say no one had been buried in that particular tomb, the women would know better. They would voice the truth.

These women who followed Jesus from Galilee had also followed him to his death and burial. Apparently there were many women. We have this from Matthew and Mark in particular. The women's fidelity to Jesus is not to be doubted since they tended to his needs during his public ministry, and also his need for their presence during the agonizing experience at Calvary.

If we turn from the death of Jesus many centuries ago to the present day, we can try to envision what would happen if Christ himself visited now. Christ is crucified continuously. We who are his disciples stand with him, present to him. There are times that we feel so helpless, so powerless, almost futile as we strive to be of service to Christ in others. We wonder what we can do to care for him in his suffering poor, in the millions and millions of refugees throughout the world, in the oppressed of every nation, oppressed in so many and in such various ways. Then we allow our thoughts to turn to the women at Calvary who loved Jesus with an intensity that must have brought pain to each one as she realized that the only help she could give to the one so loved was simply her presence and her prayers.

Jesus had brought these women to his service by the mere power of his love for them, his charisma, his sharing of life, his teaching about the kingdom of God both here and hereafter. The women were committed to being his disciples. Now the most that Mary and the women with her were able to do for him at Calvary was to be present. We so often are in that kind of situation. Yet we must not allow ourselves to think that there is nothing we can do. We must remind ourselves that presence is love in person. There is within each of us a power that is greater than self, the power of the Spirit of God communicating his strength and love to the one in need. Without our presence, the power of the Holy Spirit in us would not be expressed to the one in need.

A further consideration allows us to understand the various ways in which we are present to another. In the instance of the women who followed Jesus, their presence was visible and physical. In the instance of our presence to the millions of people in need throughout the world today, we turn to prayer and are present in our manner of holding up to God the needs of our brothers and sisters wherever they may be.

We contemporary disciples of Jesus know that there are times we can do something to bring about change, but that there are other times when we feel helpless, when all we can do is simply be with the person in need, either in our physical presence or through remembrance in prayer. When we feel utterly helpless, then we are at our weakest, unable to better a situation or to help a person. But we know that when we are weak God looks upon us with love and compassion. Then indeed he responds to our prayers that rise from the pain in our hearts. Sometimes our prayer is standing at the foot of the cross, being present to the beloved. This is a hard lesson to learn, but the women at Calvary speak to us of this. This is part of the cost of discipleship.

14
After the Resurrection
Women Are the First to See the Risen Christ

This final scene in our reflections is naturally one of great joy. Once again, because of the length of the readings, it will be impossible for all three accounts to be narrated. Matthew's account will be used. The account is also found in Mark 16:1-8, 9-13 (the skip in verses will be explained later); and in Luke 24:1-11.

After the sabbath, as the first day of the week was dawning, Mary Magdalene and the other Mary came to see the tomb. And behold, there was a great earthquake; for an angel of the Lord descended from heaven, approached, rolled back the stone, and sat upon it. His appearance was like lightning and his clothing was white as snow. The guards were shaken with fear of him and became like dead men. Then the angel said to the women in reply, ''Do not be afraid! I know that you are seeking Jesus the crucified. He is not here, for he has been raised just as he said. Come and see the place where he lay. Then go quickly and tell his disciples, 'He has been raised from the dead, and he is going before you to Galilee; there you will see him.' Behold, I have told you.'' Then they went away quickly from the tomb, fearful yet overjoyed, and ran to announce this to his disciples. And behold, Jesus met them on their way and greeted them. They approached, embraced his feet, and did him homage. Then Jesus said to them, "Do not be afraid. Go tell my brothers to go to Galilee, and there they will see me" (Matthew 28:1-10).

Once again we need to call attention to the similarities and the differences in the three accounts of the Synoptic Gospels. All three Evangelists agree that it was the first day of the week; that Mary Magdalene and another or others came to the tomb; that the stone was rolled back; that the women were given a message to carry to the other disciples; and that the women's story was not believed by the men.

The discrepancies are rather minor compared with the similarities. Matthew speaks of an angel of the Lord descending from heaven and rolling back the stone; Luke reports that two men in dazzling garments were there. Mark says the stone had been rolled back and a young man was sitting in the tomb.

Commentators do not agree about the ending of the original Passion narrative in Mark. This is the reason we gave Mark's account as verses 1-8 and 9-13. Their question is, did Mark's original account include an apparition scene? Was it added later? If the longer ending is accepted, Jesus appeared to Mary Magdalene who then went to announce the good news to his followers. Mark writes in the longer ending, "When he had risen, early on the first day of the week, he appeared first to Mary Magdalene, out of whom he had driven seven demons. She went and told his companions who were mourning and weeping. When they heard that he was alive and had been seen by her, they did not believe" (Mark 16:9-11).

The Resurrection of the Lord is not described in any version. We do not know, specifically, what a resurrection is like so it could never be captured in words.

Think about your own life and ask yourself how often you have died in the course of daily living, whether it be from rejection, insult, or any of the ways we know how to hurt each other. Still, didn't you rise to new life again? Sometimes we may wonder whether we ever will rise from the blow that "killed" us. We can be killed by a look or by a word, by being ignored or devalued. Sometimes we are killed by other people's sorrows that afflict us — death of a loved one, injury to someone dear to us, mental and psychological illnesses of persons who are meaningful to us. When this happens our joy in living is gone. We wonder if we will ever laugh again, ever rid ourselves of the heavy stone that has replaced our heart.

We walk through a dark place in life and suddenly, without any warning, we find ourselves again in the light of the sun. We can smile and laugh and enjoy life once more. We have risen from our death, but how or why the dark time happened is still a mystery. We know of our own resurrections after the fact. Perhaps that is why no one could have described the Resurrection of the Lord. Who believed that it would happen? We have already read in Mark that the disciples refused to believe the women. Luke says, "Then they returned from the tomb and announced all these things to the eleven and to all the others. The women were Mary Magdalene, Joanna, and Mary the mother of James; the others who accompanied them also told this to the apostles, but their story seemed like nonsense and they did not believe them" (Luke 24:8-11).

How ironic that Jesus first appeared, not to his apostles — the Twelve (now the Eleven) — but to Mary Magdalene and other women. His message, as told by Matthew, was, "Do not be afraid."

With the report of the women at the tomb, we come to the end of reflections on Jesus' direct encounters with women. What can we understand from this scene? Just this — that disciples of all times, like the women in these accounts, revere the Lord. Because of their love and reverence, Jesus will show himself to them. We who live close to two thousand years after the Resurrection know "that the Son of Man must be delivered into the hands of sinful men and be crucified, and on the third day rise again."

We disciples of the risen Lord cry out with joy:

> He is alive!
> > He is with us!
> In him we live,
> > In him we are raised to new life,
> No longer dead but alive.
> > He is with us.
> His message is clear:
> > Peace!
> Do not be afraid!

Also by Sister Adolorata Watson

MARY, WOMAN OF FAITH
By highlighting the events of Mary's life recorded in the Gospels, these sensitive, contemporary reflections can help you know Mary as both a real person and the most Blessed Mother. **$1.50**

Other Books for Women

WOMEN OF VALOR
by Alicia von Stamwitz

This book tells the stories of unusual saints like Saint Mary Bartholomea Bagnes who suffered a nervous breakdown, and Saint Margaret of Cortona who had an illegitimate child. These seven short biographies show that saints have suffered the same conflicts and temptations everyone else deals with and how they still reached for holiness despite the odds. **$1.95**

DOWN GOSPEL BYWAYS
18 Stories of People Who Met Jesus
by Mary Terese Donze, A.S.C.

Grandfather Simeon, who held the infant Jesus . . . Magdalene, who found a Savior . . . Simon, who carried the Cross for Christ. Meet them and others in these short stories that help you read between the lines of Matthew, Mark, Luke, and John to find real people touched by Christ's life. **$2.95**

MERRY MARY MEDITATIONS
by Bernadette McCarver Snyder

This book of brief meditations offers some new, unique, and wonderful ways to look at Mary . . . as marmalade, maestro, macrame, and more! The author chips away the marble from our statue images of her to reveal a real person — and a true friend. **$2.95**

Order from your local bookstore or write to:
Liguori Publications, Box 060, Liguori, Missouri 63057
*Please add 75¢ for postage and handling for first
item ordered and 25¢ for each additional item.)*